Explore

Fort William &

Glen Nevis

————

A Detailed Tourist Guide to
Fort William & Glen Nevis

————

BRIAN SMAILE

Walk Guides   **17 WALKS IN GLEN NEVIS**

ISBN1-903568-05-6

THE GREAT GLEN WAY

ISBN 1-903568-13-7

THE SCOTTISH COAST TO COAST WALK

ISBN 0-9526900-8-X

THE NATIONAL 3 PEAKS WALK

ISBN 1-903568-24-2

JOHN O'GROATS TO LANDS END

ISBN 1-903568-18-8

THE YORKSHIRE DALES TOP TEN

ISBN 0-9526900-5-5

THE DERBYSHIRE TOP TEN

ISBN 1-903568-03-X

THE COMPLETE ISLE OF WIGHT COASTAL FOOTPATH

ISBN 0-9526900-6-3

ISLE OF WIGHT, NORTH TO SOUTH – EAST TO WEST

ISBN1-903568-07-2

THE YORKSHIRE 3 PEAKS WALK

ISBN 1-903568-22-6

THE YORKSHIRE 3 PEAKS WALK SKETCH MAP & ROUTE GUIDE

ISBN 1-903568-24-4

THE LANCASHIRE TRAIL

ISBN 1-903568-10-2

THE LYKE WAKE WALK GUIDE

ISBN 1-903568-14-5

SHORT WALKS IN THE LAKE DISTRICT

ISBN 1-903568-20-X

Cycling Guide   **LANDS END TO JOHN O'GROATS**

ISBN 1-903568-11-0

Tourist Guide   **TOURIST GUIDE TO VARADERO, CUBA**

ISBN 1-903568-08-0

**The above can be obtained from bookshops or direct from the address
below. See web site for details. www.chall-pub.fsnet.co.uk**

EXPLORE – FORT WILLIAM & GLEN NEVIS

ISBN 1-903568-25-0

First Edition 2005

CHALLENGE PUBLICATIONS

7, EARLSMERE DRIVE, BARNSLEY. S71 5HH

THE AUTHOR
BRIAN SMAILES

Holds the record for the fastest 4 and 5 continuous crossings of the Lyke Wake Walk over the North York Moors. He completed the 210miles over rough terrain on 5 crossings in June 1995 taking 85hours and 50minutes. In 2004 he completed his 49th crossing.

His most recent venture was to walk from John O'Groats to Lands End, completing it in August 2003 in 34 days. In August 2001 he cycled from Lands End to John O'Groats, a journey of over 900 miles in 6 days 13 hours 18 minutes. This involved carrying food, clothing and tent, and was completed without support between both ends.

Brian lectures on outdoor pursuit courses and between these travels extensively on walking expeditions and projects around Great Britain.

Long distance running and canoeing are other sports he enjoys, completing 25 marathons and canoeing the Caledonian Canal 3 times.

Having travelled extensively throughout the UK, Europe and the Caribbean, Brian has recently been writing international travel guides to enable the holidaymaker to access the world with ease and enjoy it as much as he does.

Brian has walked the mountains and glens throughout the area. In compiling this 1st edition of Explore – Fort William & Glen Nevis, the area still holds as much pleasure now as it did the first time he visited.

ACKNOWLEDGEMENTS

It is with thanks to the following people for assistance, that this book has been published: -

Derek Walker
Pam Smailes

Photographs - Brian Smailes.

Brian Smailes is identified as author of this book in accordance with Copyright Act 1988.
No part of this publication may be reproduced by any means without prior permission in writing from the publisher.

First Published 2005
ISBN 1-903568-25-0

Published by Challenge Publications, 7, Earlsmere Drive, Ardsley, Barnsley, S71 5HH.
www.chall-pub.fsnet.co.uk

Printed by Dearne Valley Printers, Wath on Dearne, Rotherham.

The information recorded in this book is believed by the author to be correct at time of publication. No liabilities can be accepted for any inaccuracies found. Anyone using this guide should refer to their map in conjunction with this book. The description of a route used is not evidence of a right of way.

CONTENTS

PHOTOGRAPHS

INTRODUCTION

Explore Fort William & Glen Nevis is a book for tourists that will enable those who have not fully explored this part of Scotland, and those on their first visit, to see all that this splendid area has to offer.

This is the area of Bonnie Prince Charlie, battles and historical splendour. It is known as the Lochaber district, which is at the south west end of the great glen and stretches from Loch Leven in the south to Loch Arkaig in the north. Since 1975 when regionalisation was introduced, areas like Morar, Ardgour, Knoydart, Ardnamurchan and Glenfinnan now all come under the umbrella of Lochaber.

Bonnie Prince Charlie raised his standard here in 1745 at the start of the Jacobite rebellion and it ended here when, as a hunted man, he was sheltered before eventually being taken to the Isle of Skye then to France.

Fort William, the largest town in the highlands, lies on the eastern banks of Loch Linnhe in the Scottish Highlands. It is the main town in the area with numerous villages around the outskirts. Lochs and mountains surround it, the most famous being Ben Nevis, the highest mountain in Scotland and the UK.

There are many hotels, B&Bs and camp/caravan sites all catering for the visitor. The locals are friendly and will give a good Scottish welcome to visitors not only from the UK but also from all over the world.

Fort William represents the start or end of the Caledonian Canal, which runs to Inverness on the east coast. Within the area there are many outdoor activity centres, which cover all manner of water sports and land-based activities.

The Tourist Information Centre in Fort William provides interesting displays of local attractions as well as general information about the area. The Glen Nevis Visitor Centre gives information about Ben Nevis and Glen Nevis area with displays of fauna and flora in the glen.

There are mountains to walk in the area, whisky distilleries to visit, cable cars and cruises to venture on. Local restaurants around Fort William offer good food. There are numerous hostelries in which to sample local ale.

Visitors will find the area around Fort William very pleasant and picturesque. Many of the buildings are stone built and the town is clean and pleasant. A wide range of shops caters for all tastes in local food and souvenirs. There are a number of outdoor shops selling maps, compasses and most outdoor equipment.

Over recent years the area has become a set for film producers with films like Braveheart, Harry Potter and Highlander being filmed here.

Travelling to Fort William by car will give some of the best views anywhere in the UK particularly travelling through Glen Coe. A rail and bus link will also transport you there from throughout the British Isles. Take a camera to give you some lasting memories.

To reduce driving and give you more actual holiday time, this book has been arranged in bands of 0-3 miles, 3-6 miles, 6-9 miles and over 9 miles from the centre of Fort William. You can organise your holiday effectively, see the sights and hear the sounds (bagpipes).

There are some excellent walks included for those who are keen walkers, and some suggested 'days out' so you can see all the area. Finally at the back of this book is useful information for attractions and amenities in the area with addresses/telephone numbers.

Enjoy your stay and Scottish welcome!

HOW TO GET THERE

Fort William lies on the eastern banks of Loch Linnhe in the western highlands.

By Road: -

From Glasgow, take the A82 through Dumbarton then by Loch Lomond to Crianlarich then on to Ballachulish and Fort William, passing through Glencoe on route. A spectacular journey by Loch Lomond and Glencoe. Stay on A82 all the way from Glasgow.

From Inverness, take the A82 heading southwest by Loch Ness directly to Fort William.

By Rail: -

From stations throughout the UK to Fort William. Check times with your local station.

By Air to: -

Glasgow Airport then coach from Glasgow to Fort William.

Inverness Airport then coach from Inverness to Fort William.

GENERAL FACTS ABOUT THE AREA

- The annual Ben Nevis race usually takes place on the 1st Saturday in September.

- Between 1881-1882 Mr Clement Wragg climbed Ben Nevis every day for two summers to record the weather before the observatory was established.

- A number of cars have successfully driven to the summit of Ben Nevis, the first in 1911 by Mr. Henry Alexander.

- Fort William is the largest town in the Highlands.

- Bonnie Prince Charlie raised his standard near here in 1745 and the first skirmishes were fought near here in the 1745 uprising at Highbridge near Spean Bridge.

- Fort William was the first town in the country to have electric streetlights.

- Whisky has been made in the local distillery here since at least 1825 and continues today.

- The world downhill mountain bike championships have been held here for the past two years at the Nevis Range. Britain's only mountain gondola system takes visitors up to 2150ft on Aonach Mor also from the Nevis range at Leanachan Forest.

- General Wade's Military Road runs throughout the area. This road was built to transport soldiers quickly from one garrison to another, similar to the Roman Roads. Driving along the A82 by Leanachan Forest, the road runs parallel with it along the edge of the forest. The narrow road through Blarmachfoldach is also the Military Road.

GENERAL INFORMATION

Parking in Fort William
There is a large pay and display car park on the left by the first roundabout as you enter the town. There is also a large car park just behind both sides of the High Street. Limited street parking is also available around the town.
There is another large car park behind the Safeway supermarket.

Parking in Glen Nevis
There is a large free car park at the Visitor Centre in Glen Nevis and a number of lay-bys along the glen. There are also car parks at various locations in Nevis Forest on your right side as you drive along the glen. A small parking area is opposite the Youth Hostel by the footbridge.
Car parks are available nearby the Lower Falls and at the end of the glen road by the Upper Falls. Again there are small lay-bys and picnic places along the glen, but take care not to park in passing places on the narrow part of the road.

Public Holidays
Are different to the English holidays at some times. Christmas Day, Boxing Day and Good Friday are usually the same. Check with information centres for other current holidays.

Currency
The currency used in Scotland is the pound. Both English and Welsh pounds are accepted, although you may be given change in Scottish pounds or Scottish notes. These are usable in England on your return from holiday.
Those visitors from abroad who require currency changing, the banks in the area are shown in the back of this book. Most banks are open Monday to Friday apart from official holidays. There are a number of cash machines in Fort William.

Restaurants

There are a variety of restaurants in the town and many of the pubs in serve meals to around 9pm but it is advisable to book as they get very busy during peak holiday periods.

Some restaurants may charge VAT on top of your bill, others include the VAT in the published price. It usually states on the menu if VAT or service charge is included.

A service charge is sometimes charged instead of tipping in some establishments, if not then you may like to leave a suitable tip for good service.

Accommodation

In Fort William and the surrounding area there are many Hotels, B&Bs, caravan and camping sites. Generally there should be no problem finding accommodation, however, at busy holiday periods it is advisable to pre-book otherwise you may be without a bed for the night.

The Tourist Information Centres can usually help in finding accommodation so it is always advisable to contact them, ideally before you visit the area, and use the 'book a bed' ahead system.

Scottish Food

Scotland is renowned for fine food and the following is a selection of the traditional dishes that visitors should sample when visiting the area.

Neeps & Tatties - This is turnip and potato mashed together and served hot.

Haggis - A traditional dish of oatmeal and barley with the 'hidden extra'. Many tales and stories have been written and told about haggis.

Scottish Kippers – Smoked to give them a unique flavour.

Venison – Traditional Scottish fayre, it can be put into pies, casseroles and even burgers.

Whisky

This is the traditional drink of Scotland and many places have whisky tasting. There are many distilleries, with the local Ben Nevis Distillery photo 1, here on the outskirts of Fort William.

There are three types of whisky, blended, grain and malt. Malt whisky is made from malted barley; grain whisky is made from maize, rye or oats. Blended whisky as the name suggests, is blended from a number of other whiskies.

A visit to a distillery to see whisky being made, then to sample it is recommended. You can usually purchase some from the distillery shop to take back home, as well as from shops in Fort William.

Entertainment in the Area

In the town centre, many of the pubs, especially in the high season have entertainment each evening. Usually it is singing of popular music or traditional Scottish music. Some establishments have accordion players who play a wide variety of Scottish tunes and you can sometimes 'sing along'. Out of season, entertainment is often held only at weekends.

Other evening entertainment in the area consists of the cinema in Fort William, or ten-pin bowling in the Nevis Centre. A cruise on the loch during the summer months provides a refreshing experience.

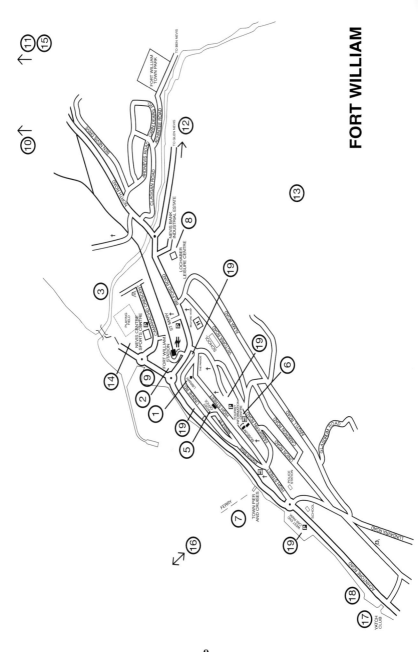

FORT WILLIAM

Key

1. Library
2. Station
3. Nevis Centre
4. The Parade
5. Post Office
6. T.I.C./Cinema/Museum
7. Town Pier
8. Leisure Centre
9. Old Fort William
10. Inverlochy Castle
11. Ben Nevis Distillery
12. Waterfalls
13. Cow Hill Mast
14. Supermarket
15. Lochaber Smelter
16. Ferry
17. Yacht Club
18. Small Park Area
19. Car Parks

Photo 1

*Ben Nevis
Distillery*

Photo 2

*Wishing Stone
in Glen Nevis*

Photo 3

*River Nevis
beside the
Visitor Centre*

11

Plate 4

View of Ben Nevis from the Caledonian Canal

Plate 5

One of the many Waterfalls in Glen Nevis

Plate 6

The Waterslide

VISITING GLEN NEVIS

Glen Nevis is situated on the outskirts of Fort William and the entrance to it is at **Nevis Bridge** just past Fort William Leisure Centre. A roundabout is beside the bridge, which can be very busy in high season. The glen is truly a place not to be missed.

Near the entrance to the glen, you see a sign on your right by the Nevis roundabout for the start or end of **The West Highland Way,** the first long distance footpath in Scotland. Look for the walkers in Glen Nevis, as they are about to finish the long walk from Milngarvie near Glasgow.

There are a number of B&Bs near the entrance to the glen. A small power station is on your right as you proceed into the glen, but like many power stations in Scotland it is quite discreet as it generates hydro-electricity.

Just past there is the 1st entrance into **Nevis Forest.** There are a number of entrances along the Glen, where walkers, mountain bikers and visitors are welcome. You are able, subject to timber operations, to walk from here to the far end of the glen through the woods. The path is generally higher up the hillside so you have good views of the glen and Ben Nevis.

Next place along the glen is the **Wishing Stone photo 2,** by the side of the road on the right, 0.9 mile from Nevis Bridge. This stone is very large and is known as Samuel's Stone or Clach Shomhairle. Park in the free car park at **Glen Nevis Visitor Centre,** or to give it its correct title **Ionad Nibheis,** which is 1.3 miles from Nevis Bridge, on the left. Walk back to view the stone and make a wish.

On the same side as the wishing stone you should see the **cemetery,** which is one of two in the area. If you go in and walk to the rear of it on the higher ground, you can read the headstone inscriptions of those unfortunate people who were killed while walking or climbing Ben Nevis. This may just prompt you to take extra care if you are about to walk up Ben Nevis yourself!

Returning to the **Visitor Centre,** this hosts displays of the fauna and flora of the glen and interprets the natural and cultural heritage of this special area. Helpful staff gives information about the glen and Ben Nevis in particular. There are maps, books and other souvenir items for sale. Rangers who are based here give visitors guidance and there is an annual programme of guided walks in the glen. Situated in a superb setting close by the **River Nevis, photo 3,** it is ideal for picnics and as a base for walking and general sightseeing of the glen. This Visitor Centre is the official starting point for walkers to ascend Ben Nevis. Ben **Nevis, photo 4,** the highest mountain in the UK is owned by the John Muir Trust, who tries to conserve the area whilst allowing walkers and climbers to explore the area.

Proceeding along the glen road, just past the visitor centre on the right side is a narrow path between fields. This path leads to the forest, but going through a 5-bar gate at the end of the short path, over a small platform footbridge and up a small embankment will take you into the **Cameron graveyard.** This is interesting as it a small graveyard for the Cameron Clan of the area, which dates from the1800's.

Returning to the road and a little further along is the main camping and caravan site in the area which is **'The Glen Nevis Camping and Caravan Park.** This 5* site is very good and spacious and can get full, but most people can be accommodated even in the high season.

Photo 7

*Steall
Falls*

Photo 8

*High Street,
Fort William*

Photo 9

*Small Park
Area*

Plate 10

Inverlochy Castle

Plate 11

View of Neptune's Staircase with Fort William in Distance

Plate 12

View of Fort William from Cow Hill

A large white house is just off the main road at the side of the Caravan Park. This is **Glen Nevis House** and it has a distinguished history. Mrs Cameron of Glen Nevis House hid in a cave further up the glen to escape government troops, but they eventually found her and tried in vain to find where she had hidden the family silver. Not being able to find it they left, but not before burning throughout the glen on their exit. The house was the headquarters of Lochiel when his 2000 soldiers laid siege to Fort William in 1746.

At the far end of the site is the **Glen Nevis Bar & Restaurant.** Here you can sit at the foothills of Ben Nevis and discuss the days activities while relaxing with a meal or drinks.

Further on is **Glen Nevis Youth Hostel.** This is popular all year round, especially with walkers. Opposite is the alternative start when ascending Ben Nevis. A footbridge gives access to the lower slopes for walkers and there is a nice flat riverbank walk on the far side to the Visitor Centre.

Now you are going into the main glen as you proceed along the winding undulating road. Nevis Forest is on your right and there are various access points all the way along and some nice walks through. Going into the forest you can ascend to a knoll on a hillside above the forest that is called **Dun Deardail.** This is an **Iron Age Fort** and it commands good views over all the area, although it may be a stiff climb for many to access it.

Near the end of the forest you come to **Achriabach** and ¼ mile further the **Lower Falls, photo 5.** Park in the car park there and visit the two bridges to see the water gushing down to the pools at the far side of the bridges. Take your camera!

Now there is an ascent to the end of the glen. Cross the bridges and continue up the single-track road. Nearing the end, look for a **water slide, photo 6,** streaming down the mountainside from your left. You can park at the end and walk back a short distance to the slide. Go between the trees and ascend to the slide with care, if you want to view this unusual sight.

Returning to the end of the glen road, look for a narrow path at the end. This will take you to **Steall Falls** and the spectacular **waterfall, photo 7,** which falls from the hillside. **See the section on best walks.**

This popular walk takes 25 minutes to get there and is worth the effort. Look down on the river gushing down between the rocks. You eventually come to a hanging valley when the narrow winding path suddenly gives way to a flat expanse of grass. The waterfall is at the far end and a **rope bridge,** which the more energetic and adventurous may like to try their skill in crossing, with care!

Your tour of Glen Nevis is not over because when returning you have splendid views of the Glen, Ben Nevis and the routes up it, and of the **River Nevis** and the picnic areas on many parts of the riverbank. Once you have visited here, like many others you will want to return.

Be sure to take some protection from the **midge,** the small fly that is well known here and throughout the country. It is generally around between early June and September.

Plate 13

Old Fort William & Start of The Great Glen Way Walk

Plate 14

Hilltop Picnic Area with Loch Linnhe in the Distance

Plate 15

Stone Circle at Corpach

Plate 16

Nevis Range & Gondola Entrance

Plate 17

Gondola Ride on Aonach Mor

Plate 18

River Kiachnish near Lundavra

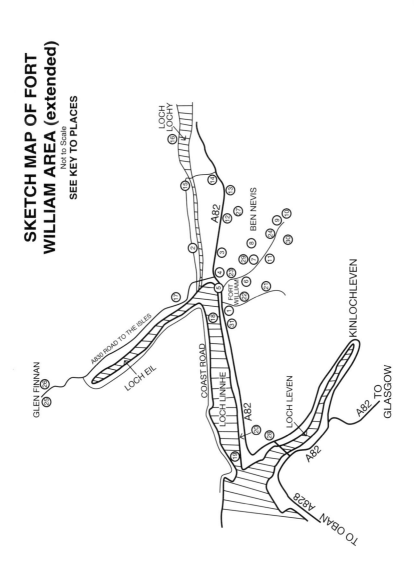

SKETCH MAP OF FORT WILLIAM AREA (extended)

Not to Scale

SEE KEY TO PLACES

LOCH LOCHY

BEN NEVIS

A82

A830 ROAD TO THE ISLES

LOCH EIL

GLEN FINNAN

COAST ROAD

LOCH LINNHE

A82

LOCH LEVEN

FORT WILLIAM

KINLOCHLEVEN

A82 TO GLASGOW

A82

TO OBAN A828

21

KEY

1. Fort William
2. Neptunes Staircase
3. Golf Club
4. Ben Nevis Distillery
5. Inverlochy Castle
6. Nevis Forest
7. Visitor Centre
8. Ben Nevis
9. Waterslide
10. Steall Falls
11. Caravan/Camping Park
12. Leanachan Forest
13. Spean Bridge
14. Commando Memorial
15. Gairlochy
16. Clan Cameron Museum
17. Treasures of the Earth
18. Ferry
19. Corran Ferry
20. Picnic Area
21. Blarmachfoldach
22. Picnic Area
23. Waterfalls
24. Waterfalls
25. Glenfinnan Monument
26. Glenfinnan Viaduct
27. Aonach Mor
28. North Ballachulish & Bridge
29. Ben Nevis Inn
30. Dun Deardail
31. Small Park Area

Plate 19

Spean Bridge Mill

Plate 20

Clan Cameron Museum, Achnacarry

Plate 21

Japanese Style Bridge, Invergloy

Plate 22

*Path to
Ben Nevis*

Plate 23

*View of the
Mountains
and
Glen Nevis
from
Ben Nevis*

Plate 24

*Near Ben Nevis
Summit*

PLACES TO VISIT

0 – 3 MILES FROM FORT WILLIAM

Fort William Centre

Here in Fort William is a busy High Street, **photo 8,** of shops and pubs. In the centre is Cameron Square with a **tourist information centre** and a small **museum.** A **cinema** (studio cinema) is tucked away to the side of the TIC for those who like to watch a film. There is a daily choice of at least two films.

During the evenings in the summer months, a **pipe band** march in the main street and this gives the true 'taste of the highlands' to visitors from all over the world. There are a number of public houses, most of which serve food. They are Crofter Bar & Restaurant, Alexandra Hotel, Nevisport Bar, Imperial Hotel Bar, West End Hotel, Volunteer Arms, Grog & Gruel, Ben Nevis Pub, and Grand Hotel Lounge Bar. Those who require banking services have the Halifax, Clydesdale Bank, Royal Bank of Scotland, Post Office and Lloyds TSB to choose from.

There are a variety of shops in the town and these include numerous gift shops, whisky shops, supermarket, takeaways and outdoor sport and clothes shops. Usually you can purchase most items needed on a holiday so you don't need to bring the kitchen sink!

A short walk back along the A82 towards Ballachulish is **Fort William Yacht Club.** If you prefer life on a boat or fancy a sail then contact the club for advice. The club is just past the small park area, which has seats looking out over the Loch. Opposite is a row of hotels and B&Bs.

West Highland Museum

Situated in Cameron Square in the centre of Fort William nearby the TIC.

This museum is world famous for its Jacobite collection including the secret portrait of Prince Charles Stuart. It has many other interesting exhibits and is worth a visit to help fully understand the history of the area. Open all year.

McTavish's Kitchen
Situated in the High Street in Fort William.
Visitors to the area, especially from abroad can experience the true taste and culture of Scotland here, either just to see the show or to eat traditional food. There are traditional songs, music and dance with piping. The evening is something the visitor will remember for many years. Open May to September.

Fort William Pier
Situated on the lower side of the town on the banks of Loch Linnhe.
Fort William Pier was built in the 19th century then sold in 1979 to Lochaber District Council. The pier was rededicated in 1989 when the restaurant was built. You can book cruises on the loch and to neighbouring islands from here. There are gatherings on the pier with live music nights and seafood barbeques. Also on the pier is Crannog Seafood Restaurant, which has a reputation for excellent food. You will recognise it by the distinctive red and white painted frontage.
A small **ferry** leaves from the pier, travelling to a jetty opposite at **Camusnagaul.** Price £1.20 adults and 50p children in 2004. You can take pedal cycles across, and it is a very nice ride around the southern shoreline of Loch Eil, back to Fort William. Camusnagaul is a place where fishing boats often anchor and fishermen ply their trade on the shore.

Putting Green – The Parade
Situated in front of Nevisport/WH Smith.
There is a small putting green on 'The Parade', where you can hire clubs and enjoy a game on this small town centre course. Beside the putting green is a bell, placed there as a bond of friendship between Dudley, Hiroshima and Fort William and to commemorate the international peace cairn on Ben Nevis summit – in the hope for a peaceful world.
Within the town green area is a statue of Domhnall Camshron Lochiel.

Picnic Site

Situated at the top of Lundavra Road, from the roundabout by the police station in Fort William, take Lundavra Road (sign) to ascend for 0.9 miles through the housing estate. Cross a cattle grid near the top and continue a short distance to a hill on the left.

At the summit by the roadside is a gate and car parking area. Inside the enclosed picnic area, **photo 14,** are picnic tables, plants and flowers. A good view of the surrounding area can be had from here.

The Jacobite Steam Train – Fort William

Situated on the edge of the town centre at the station beside Safeway supermarket.

This train journey from Fort William to Mallaig has been described as one of the great train journeys of the world. The route crosses the Glenfinnan Viaduct, passes Loch Shiel and the Jacobite monument before reaching Arisaig then Mallaig. Scenes for the Harry Potter films were shot here and on the Glenfinnan Viaduct, so you may already recognise the train and other areas on route. Open June – October.

Small Park Area - Fort William

Situated on the banks of Loch Linnhe 0.6 miles from the centre by the A82 on Achintore Road just before entering the town on the west side, **photo 9.**

This small open park area can easily be missed, but an extended walk along 'the front' on the A82 southwest out of town towards the yacht club will lead to this park. There are seats and fine views over the loch. Depending on time of year, the flowerbeds may be in full bloom, which makes the short walk along even more worthwhile.

Waterfalls - River Nevis

Reached by taking A82 to Nevis roundabout. Take Inverness road then 1st right turn after roundabout onto Claggan Road. Follow it around then right onto Achintee

Road. As you draw near the sports grounds, look for parking on your right. Walk behind a house on the right and on the grass path to the river and waterfalls, 1½ mile from Fort William centre.

This is a nice spot for a picnic and to relax by the river. It is a favourite place of local people who can often be seen jumping off the rocks into the pools, but take care. Continue along this single-track road will take you to the lower slopes of Ben Nevis. Where the road stops is also the start of a path that leads to Ben Nevis. A pub here called the Ben Nevis Inn is a welcome stopping place offering nice meals. Relax in this highland pub and enjoy good views of the glen from here.

Inverlochy Castle
Situated 1½ miles along the A82 heading NW on the Inverness road, turn left before the Victoria Bridge traffic lights and follow the sign and short winding road round to the castle where there is free parking opposite.

A good example of a Scottish castle, **photo 10,** this is one of the few to survive largely unaltered since before the wars of independence 1296-1357. The castle was built by the powerful Comyn family around 1280 but only occupied by them until 1308. After being abandoned it was used sporadically over the centuries. It was the centre of the lordship with public and private chambers. At the time of writing this book, the castle was undergoing restoration. The River Lochy is on the far side of the castle where originally there was access directly onto the river. Battles were fought close by in 1431 and 1645 and the immediate area is steeped in history.

Old Burial Ground - Inverlochy
Situated 1½ mile along A82 (see Inverlochy Castle directions). After turning off A82, look for the burial ground on left on a small rise in a field. Park on road and enter through a small kissing gate there.

This burial ground has graves dating from early 1800. Nearby there is a good viewpoint from a small mound.

Caol Village

Situated just off the A830 between the traffic lights at Victoria Bridge and the Caledonian Canal.

This village, which was built after the Second World War is quite large, supports old and new houses, and has pubs and shops. It also has a nice walk around the perimeter of the village, which is actually the route of the Great Glen Way. The route takes you alongside the River Lochy, by Loch Linnhe then alongside the Caledonian Canal at its entrance, up to Banavie Station. When planning your excursion to this area, you may want to incorporate this walk with a visit to Neptune's Staircase, the flight of locks near Banavie Station.

Banavie

Situated on A830 just to the left of the canal by Banavie Station and just to the right on the far side.

After crossing the canal, turn right and follow the road round to the car park on the right. A small housing estate with mainly modern houses. Banavie is famous for Neptune's Staircase, which is not to be missed. The loch-keepers houses are the original houses which were built when the canal was built around 1822.

Caledonian Canal (Neptune's Staircase)

Situated approximately 3 miles from Fort William, follow the A82 out of Fort William to the traffic lights joining with the A830 to Mallaig (road to the Isles). Turn left on the A830 continue until you cross the canal bridge then turn first right. Follow the road around the bend to a large car park beside the canal at Neptune's Staircase, which is the flight of 8 locks near the start of the canal.

At this place you have good views of Ben Nevis and Loch Linnhe, **photo 11.** Flanked by the magnificent scenery of the Scottish Highlands, the canal links a chain of natural lochs to form the most beautiful waterway in Europe. Its highest point is 106ft above sea level at Loch Oich and was completed in 1822 during the aftermath of the Jacobite rebellions.

The canal was engineered by Scotsman Thomas Telford. Its early role was to provide shelter for French privateers, but it enjoyed commercial success in the 1880's. The canal is used in modern times by many pleasure cruisers and yachts. Occasionally you may see large boats passing through the loch, which only just fit.

The route of the canal is along the Great Glen, and it passes through Loch Lochy and Loch Ness before finishing (or starting) at Inverness. It is 60 miles in length and passes through 22 miles of actual canal cutting. The speed limit on the canal is 6 miles per hour and it generally takes around 14 hours passage time to travel from one end to the other and negotiate the 29 locks between.

Ben Nevis Distillery

Situated just past the traffic lights on A82 by Victoria Bridge on right side. A car park is reached through the gates at the entrance.

The distillery, **photo 1,** was established in 1825 and has seen the visit of Queen Victoria in 1848. The three million litres of whisky made in this distillery each year uses the water from the Coire Leis and Coire Na Ciste, drawing it off the burn below. Visitors to the distillery are taken on a tour and shown how whisky is produced. There is a small café, and a picture gallery near the entrance, depicting the history of the famous whisky and with interesting photographs, facts and figures of Ben Nevis. It is open all year, times vary.

Fort William Golf Club

Situated on the A82 Inverness road in the shadow of Ben Nevis. Continue past the traffic lights joining with the A830 and the golf club is on the right just past the lights and approximately 2 miles from Fort William.

An 18-hole course of 6217 yards, par 72 and a mixture of testing holes, but don't worry if you have forgotten your clubs as you can hire them. Day tickets are available here where you can play golf at the foothills of Ben Nevis!

Cow Hill Mast

Situated just up Lundavra Road from the centre of Fort William is one of the access routes to Cow Hill Mast. From the roundabout beside the police station in Fort William; turn left to ascend Lundavra Road. Continue right up to a cattle grid and the end of the housing estate. Just beside the cattle grid is a gate on your left leading along a path to the mast. (**Alternative route to Cow Hill Mast, see best walks section**).

This viewpoint overlooking Fort William, **photo 12,** and Loch Linnhe is another walk not to be missed. Wear warm clothing, as it can be cold and windy on top of the hill. Don't forget your camera. The views of Loch Linnhe and surrounding area will speak for themselves. There is a race to Cow Hill mast around the 12th July. Check with the TIC for current date. **See section on best walks.**

Old Fort William

Situated on the main road near the Safeway supermarket beside the roundabout.

The fort, **photo 13,** built in 1690 by Hugh MacKay and named after the king at that time, now consists of only walls alongside Loch Linnhe but the outline of the fort can be seen. Jacobite supporters held the garrison at Fort William under siege in 1746 for six weeks. Next to the walls is the start of the **Great Glen Way, photo 13,** a 73 mile walk to Inverness, which is very popular. It is marked by a stone, situated close by the old castle walls.

Inverlochy

Situated just past the Nevis Bridge roundabout on the left of the A82.

The relatively modern village of Inverlochy built in the 1900's and consisting of mainly houses and some shops, sits at the entrance to the River Lochy and close by Inverlochy Castle. There is a short walk along the riverbank from Inverlochy to nearby the castle.

Aluminium Works (known as the Lochaber Smelter)

Situated just off the A82 at Inverlochy 1 mile from Fort William centre.

You will probably see the long water pipes on the mountainside of the hydroelectric scheme, which powers the plant. The factory was originally opened in 1930 but rebuilt and reopened in 1981. There is a water chute or channel for the fast flowing water, which can be viewed nearby Inverlochy Castle as it flows into the River Lochy and it is worth a visit just to see.

Achintee by Claggan

Situated about 3 miles from Fort William, access is gained by turning right off the A82 just after crossing Nevis Bridge roundabout and following the winding road through the small industrial area then housing estate before turning right onto a narrow road leading into the glen on the left side of the River Nevis.

At the end of the narrow road is a place called the Ben Nevis Inn, a former barn that after conversion is now a pub with a bunkhouse underneath. As well as providing good ale and food, it affords views of Glen Nevis and the foothills of Ben Nevis. It is an extremely welcoming port of call after returning from a long walk up Ben Nevis!

3 – 6 MILES FROM FORT WILLIAM

Corpach Village

Situated off the A830 just over the Caledonian Canal on left and right side of the road. Follow the A82 then the A830 road to the isles, signposted.

This village stretches for approx. 2 miles, and over looks Loch Eil. Its name is from the Gaelic words, 'place of the bodies'. When a person died and wanted to be buried on Iona, the bodies were left here before being taken to the island.

Here at Corpach, you will find the picturesque entrance to the Caledonian Canal. Access is gained by turning 2nd left off the A830 after the canal. Follow the road past the village hall and into the large open area by the white painted loch keeper's house and office buildings on the right. You can walk around the entrance of the canal and there are particularly good views of Ben Nevis and Loch Linnhe to be had from here looking across the canal.

An interesting place to visit in Corpach is the standing stones, **photo 15,** beside the village hall. This is only yards from the entrance to the Caledonian Canal and you can easily walk to it. The rocks from the Western Highlands are displayed in a circle and Kilmally Council built it to commemorate the Queen's Golden Jubilee. There is a small garden, tree and cairn placed there by the children of the area in 2002.

Also in Corpach on the A830 is the Treasures of the Earth Centre. Displayed here are gemstones and crystals along with nuggets of gold and silver as well as many other types of stone and fossils, many illuminated to enhance their beauty.

Nevis Range - Torlundy

Situated 6 miles from Fort William just off A8, Leanachan Forest is home to the Gondola ride. Turn right off Inverness road following signs, onto the forest access road and continue to car park beside gondola.

The **Nevis Range, photo 16,** situated in **Leanachan Forest** is an all year round attraction offering a mountain experience to people from all walks of life. It incorporates a downhill mountain bike course, a gondola ride of up to 2150ft on Aonach Mor, beside Ben Nevis, and ski runs in the winter. The Nevis range was constructed in 1989, and the gondola can carry up to 1500 people per hour at any one time.

A trip on the **mountain gondola, photo 17,** to the top especially in the summer is highly recommended. It runs every day subject to weather and is suitable for people of all ages and most wheelchair users. Wear warm clothes if going to the summit on the gondola, as it can be cold or windy at times. At the top is a restaurant and bar, shop and discovery centre. The views towards the glens and lochs, highlands and islands from the top are stunning.

Other activities, which are gaining popularity, are **paragliding** and **hand gliding.** This is done by ascending on the gondola and taking off from an altitude of 650m. Those who are interested can make enquiries from the Nevis Range. The **downhill cycling track** is home to Britain's only world-class downhill track with gondola access. It is 3km long and descends 2000ft back to the car park. A route for the experienced and not the feint-hearted, the top cyclists completes it in around 4 minutes. Much of **Aonach Mor** is designated as a site of special scientific interest.

Back at the bottom there are 25 miles of forest tracks to explore on foot or bike. Several **forest walks** start and finish in the car park, with one of the most popular being the 45 minute River Lundy walk. Maps are available from the ticket office at the car park. Cycles can be hired both in Fort William and at the Nevis Range main building.

Lundavra/Blarmachfoldach

Situated at the end of a narrow minor road. At the A82 roundabout beside the police station in Fort William, ascend Lundavra Road and continue on the narrow undulating road through Blarmachfoldach. Nearing the far end, you pass the entrance to the West Highland Way, continue to the houses at Lundavra. Return by same route. This excursion is very nice with good views of Lochs, forest, river and moorland, **photo 18.**

6 – 9 MILES FROM FORT WILLIAM

Picnic Site
Situated 6.6 miles out of Fort William on the A82 heading back towards Ballachulish, or right side overlooking Loch Linnhe.

This is a nice area for a picnic with picnic tables, parking and excellent views over Loch Linnhe.

Corran Ferry to Ardgour
Situated 8.5 miles from Fort William on A82 towards Ballachulish at the side of Loch Linnhe.

This short ferry ride across Loch Linnhe, has truly astounding scenery, and is not to be missed.

If you travel one-way across then at the far side turn right and head up the side of Loch Linnhe on the coastal road on the A861. Follow it all the way around Loch Linnhe then Loch Eil before reaching the 'road to the isles' A830. Turn right following signs back to Fort William.

Total distance all round is about 46 miles but you may only want a ride across to Ardgour and back.

North Ballachulish
Situated just off A82 on the Glasgow road and before the bridge over the entrance to Loch Leven.

By the side of Loch Leven at the slipway in this small village. An old ferry crossed to South Ballachulish at the far side before the bridge was built in 1975. Now, the modern road by-passes the main part of the village and you have good views of Loch Linnhe as you travel on the A82 to Fort William.

Following the minor road through the village of houses, small hotels and B&Bs then along the side of the loch for 9 miles takes you to **Kinlochleven.** The village, which was formerly called Kinlochbeg on one side of the river, and Kinlochmore on the other became known as Kinlochleven.

An aluminium production plant was built and a dam constructed in the hills to the east, which produces hydro-electricity via a power station. At the far end of the loch there is 'The Aluminium Story' visitor centre. It contains a display about how a community used hydroelectric power to produce aluminium. Another 7 miles takes you to the village of Glencoe.

Once at the main A82 road, you can return to Fort William, stopping off at the gift shops, information centre and coffee shops on the way back.

The whole drive affords more excellent scenery all the way round and across the lochs with places to stop for picnics and photographs.

In Ballachulish is Dragons Tooth Golf Course, a 9-hole pay and play course with refreshments available in the clubhouse afterwards.

Spean Bridge

Situated on the A82 Inverness road 8½ miles from Fort William. Turn right into large car park by the woollen mill. Spean Bridge took its name from the bridge built by Thomas Telford in 1819. A previous bridge built by General Wade in 1736 can still be seen at Highbridge, a little further away. The first battles of the 1745 uprising took place at Highbridge.

At Spean Bridge you will find a Post Office, guesthouses, a TIC, hotel, supermarket and a well-stocked mill shop, **photo 19.** The Spean Bridge Mill shop has whisky tasting, Scottish knitwear and a trace your ancestry database. It is an interesting place to visit and a good stopping place for a coffee. There is a golf course here at Spean Bridge where visitors are welcome.

9 MILES PLUS FROM FORT WILLIAM

Glen Albyn/Glen Mor Circular Tour

Situated on the A830, cross the Caledonian Canal and take first right on B8004, a minor road behind Neptune's Staircase. Continue along glen to a right turn to Gairlochy. Follow this road back to the main A82 Inverness road then turn right back to Fort William.

Taking this road will give you a pleasant excursion for approximately 18 miles through picturesque countryside. There are forest walks and cycle routes in Glen Loy. When you see the forest on your left at Glen Loy, there is a nice restaurant on your right side. Just past Glen Loy forest is a turning right to Gairlochy and if you cross over the canal you can stop just over the far side for photographs.

Clan Cameron Museum - Achnacarry

Situated approximately 4 miles from Gairlochy. Take the A82 to the junction of A830 and turn left. Cross the Caledonian Canal and take first right on B8004, a minor road behind Neptune's Staircase. Continue along glen on the minor road, staying on it to Achnacarry. Signposted. This is a pleasant trip of about 18 miles, returning part way on same route.

This small museum, **photo 20,** created in 1989, tells the story of the clan and its involvement in the 1745 rising; Bonnie Prince Charlie's refuge, Jacobite artefacts, clan and regimental history. It also has some commando mementos because commandos trained at Achnacarry Castle and in the surrounding area. Although small, the museum has a lot of history of the area.

There are some nice walks around the area here, one of the most famous being 'The Dark Mile'. This route was first mentioned in The Jacobite Trilogy and was also used as a training area/route by the commandos in the last war. A waterfall and large pool at the end of the Dark Mile was used as a film location in Rob Roy. A detailed description of the route and its history is available inside the Clan Cameron Museum. Open April to October.

Achnacarry Castle – beside Clan Cameron Museum
This is the hereditary seat of the Clan Cameron. It was invaded after 1745 by the Duke of Cumberland's troops. It was occupied by commando troops in 1942 where they trained in the area.

Commando Memorial
Situated on the A82 Inverness road, a short distance from Spean Bridge on the hillside.
A prominent memorial, for the commandos who fought in the last war and who trained in the area, overlooking Lochaber It was built in 1952 and unveiled by the Queen Mother. There is ample parking here at this popular place, which provides a good stopping point when touring in this area.

Glenfinnan Monument
Situated just off the A830 at Glenfinnan 15 miles from Fort William on the road known as the 'road to the isles'.
This monument erected by Alexander MacDonald replaced an original monument dedicated to the memory of those who supported Bonnie Prince Charlie in 1745. The Jacobite uprising began in Glenfinnan in 1745 when Bonnie Prince Charlie raised his standard here. The monument stands at the head of Loch Shiel commanding a good view along the glen and it has a stone figure of Bonnie Prince Charlie on the top.
This place is very popular, with a visitor centre, which tells the story of the Jacobite campaign of 1745. Nearby is a craft shop with a picnic area and a large car park. Other attractions there include **loch cruises, National Trust property, railway museum** with restored railway cars and station, hill walking and film set location. Films made around here were Harry Potter, Highlander, Monarch of the Glen and Rockface. **Glenfinnan Railway Viaduct,** built in 1901, is well known from the Harry Potter films. You can take a ride on the steam train just like Harry Potter! The route takes you from Fort William along the shore of Loch Eil, passing Glenfinnan then on to Mallaig.

Japanese Style Footbridge (Invergloy)

Situated on the left side of A82 Inverness road at Invergloy, just as you approach Loch Lochy. Look for it between the trees on left next to East Lodge.

I have included this bridge because it stands out as rather unusual, **photo 21.** You can incorporate this visit with perhaps a visit to Fort Augustus, which is further along the Great Glen.

SUGGESTED DAYS OUT

The following suggested outings are arranged for convenience into areas, and take in many of the places mentioned previously in this book. However, not all places have been included, only those I feel are the main ones. On some days you may want to enjoy some of the walks mentioned in this book, which are all worth doing and very rewarding when you reach the top or complete a walk.

Day 1 - Glen Nevis

Start by calling at the **Visitor Centre** and read about the history of the glen and the area. Walk by the river to the **suspension bridge** then through the car park and cross to the **wishing stone, photo 2,** and return to the car.

Drive along the glen, stopping for coffee at the **café** or **Glen Nevis bar and restaurant.** Continue along the glen to the **Lower Falls** car park and walk to the bridges over the river to see the **waterfalls.**

Continue now, ascending the narrow road to the **Upper Falls** car park. Look for the **waterslide, photo 6,** on the left behind the trees near the top, and walk the short distance back down the road to it. Ascend through the trees to the waterslide for photographs then return to the car park. Take the path at the end of the car park to **Steall Falls, photo 7,** a very worthwhile and popular walk. *See route in walks section.*

Return back along the glen and stop near the Youth Hostel. Walking across the footbridge then turning left will give you a nice **flat short walk** to the suspension bridge further up by the Visitor Centre. Follow the path through and onto the road, walking back to the Youth Hostel and your car.

Drive to **Nevis Bridge roundabout** and turn into the gift shop car park by the West Highland Way sign. Here you have **whisky tasting** and a wide variety of gifts.

Day 2 - Corran Ferry/Ardgour & Glenfinnan

Leaving Fort William, take the A82 towards Ballachulish and follow signs to **Corran Ferry.** This short journey across the Corran Narrows of Loch Linnhe, to **Ardgour,** is not to be missed for spectacular scenery. Leaving the ferry on the opposite side, turn right and follow the coastal road A861 all the way round to **Kinlocheil.** You may be able to have a coffee at Ardgour before leaving. On the way back there are good views across Loch Linnhe of Fort William and Ben Nevis. You may like to take a picnic, weather permitting and admire the views.

At the junction, turn left onto the A830 towards **Glenfinnan.** Park in the main car park. You can visit the **monument** and **visitor centre** as well as the **railway museum, Glenfinnan Viaduct,** and the **film locations** nearby of Harry Potter, Highlander and Monarch of the Glen.

After this lengthy visit, turn back towards Fort William on the A830 and follow signs taking you back into Fort William.

Day 3 - Spean Bridge and Fort Augustus

Leaving Fort William on the A82 heading towards Inverness, stay on A82 to **Spean Bridge.** Turn right into the car park, **photo 19.** Here is a **woollen mill** where you can sample whisky, buy clothing and other gifts.

Nearby is a **visitor centre** which also has gifts and souvenirs, a **small supermarket** and a **post office.**

Leaving Spean Bridge, turn right from the car park and head towards Fort Augustus. A short distance further you come to the **commando memorial.** Turn left into the car park to visit the memorial.

Return to the A82 and continue towards Fort Augustus. A few miles further on this road you come to **Loch Lochy.** Just as you approach it, look for a narrow **footbridge** on the left at a slight bend. A little further on is a nice **café** on the right where you can park and enjoy a meal or drink.

Back on the A82 continue along the side of Loch Lochy and at the end of the loch is **Laggan Locks.** Turn left on a slight bend onto the short gravel access track taking you to the car park by the lock. It is very nice here and you may get some photographs of the boats going through the lock. Just past Laggan, you come to a swing bridge over the canal where it enters Loch Oich. Here there is a good view of some holiday homes on the far side of the loch. Just past the bend in the road, there is a monument called **'Well of the Seven Heads'.** This depicts events from the Keppoch murders. The inscription on it is written in four languages. **Fort Augustus** is 10 miles further on. This town was named after William Augustus, Duke of Cumberland, is a very popular stopping place for visitors. There are cafés and bars, shops, and a TIC. The most interesting feature however in Fort Augustus is the **flight of five locks,** which takes the canal into Loch Ness. Park in the car park by the TIC and visit the gift shop by the fuel station.

Cross the road by the canal swing bridge and walk down the street to the entrance into Loch Ness and admire the view. Returning, walk up by the flight of locks and watch the boats passing through. You may like to visit the other gift shops nearby. A butchers shop beside the flight of locks produces their own haggis, which I know to be very nice.

There was once a fort in the village but it was given to the Catholic Benedictine Order for an Abbey and School on the site, which was completed in 1882.

Return to Fort William by the same route on the A82. You may like to stop in a lay-by on the way back to admire the views along **Loch Oich and Loch Lochy.**

Day 4 - Neptune's Staircase, Glen Mor & Gairlochy

Leave Fort William on the A82 towards Inverness, and at the junction with the A830, turn left. Continue along and cross the Caledonian Canal. Take the 1st right turn after the canal onto the minor road A8004. Just after the bend, you come to a car park on the right where you can park and walk across to the **flight of locks** called **Neptune's Staircase.** There are good views of Ben Nevis from here, **photo 11.**

Leaving this car park, continue along the minor road, which has views of the Caledonian Canal down in the glen on your right. This is a pleasant run through woodland and undulating hillsides. As you reach **Glen Loy,** a large forest there has walks and **cycle tracks** to use and you can park also.

Eventually you come to a right turning to Gairlochy. Do not turn here but continue on to Achnacarry where there is a sign pointing to the **Clan Cameron Museum, photo 20.** This place is interesting as it depicts a lot of the history of the area. Just past the museum is **Achnacarry Castle.** This was invaded after 1745 by the Duke of Cumberland's troops; then in 1942 it was a base for commandos.

Return along the road you came on and there is a turning a few miles along on the left. This takes you to **Gairlochy.** Cross the canal again and you may want to stop to admire the view by the canal. Drive along the winding road and continue past the houses to the junction of the A82 by the **commando memorial.**

Turn right and continue along the main road back to Fort William, passing **Spean Bridge** on the way.

Day 5 - Leanachan Forest & Gondola Ride

Leave Fort William on the A82 Inverness road. Stay on this road passing the golf club until you come to a sign for the forest. Turn right there, taking you to the car park by the **Nevis Range, photo 16.** From here you have a choice of a number of activities. There are **walks** and numerous mountain and **forest trails, cycle tracks** and a **downhill route** and **paragliding** (by pre-booking).

The main attraction here is the **gondola ride,** which takes you up to 2150ft on **Aonach Mor, photo 17,** beside Ben Nevis. From the top the views are excellent and the air fresh and cold so wear some warm clothing. Don't forget to take a camera. You can walk to panoramic viewpoints at the top and visit the restaurant and bar. A **Mountain Discovery Centre** is there for a closer look at the wildlife and landscape.

You return by the same route back to the bottom.

This is a good day out and an exhilarating experience.

Returning back to Fort William, continue to just before the traffic lights at the junction with the A830. This is the **Ben Nevis Distillery, photo 1,** and if you have not seen how whisky is made then now is your chance. In the entrance is some interesting information, facts and figures about the history of Ben Nevis and how cars have reached the summit. **Guided tours** of the distillery run all year at regular intervals and there is the customary tasting session. A cafe is also situated inside, offering food and drinks. This is another place worth visiting.

On your way back into Fort William, just before you reach Nevis Bridge roundabout, turn left at the last road before the roundabout and follow the road through an industrial area and by houses then turn right onto a narrowing road leading to **Achintee** and the **Ben Nevis Inn** at the very end of the road. From here you have views of the Ben Nevis path and Glen Nevis. The pub offers food and drinks and is a welcome refreshment stop for many people returning from a walk up Ben Nevis.

FILM & TV LOCATIONS IN THE AREA

Throughout the Lochaber area, the scenery is stunning and the ideal location for many well known films including Rob Roy, Braveheart, Harry Potter and Highlander. You can drive along Glen Nevis and probably recognise some of the locations used in Braveheart and Rockface.
If you fancy being a film buff for a day then go and visit some of the places. The children especially will enjoy a visit to Glenfinnan and perhaps a ride on the Harry Potter train!

Ballachulish - 14 miles from Fort William
Around this area the film Kidnapped was filmed in 1960 and shots of Ballachulish Bridge and Loch Leven also feature in Rockface and Catch me a Spy.

Ardgour – 8 miles from Fort William across ferry
Large amounts of the film Kidnapped was shot around this small village and there are shots of the lighthouse in the Corran Narrows.

Glenfinnan – 15 miles from Fort William
This is a film producers paradise with Harry Potter and the Chamber of Secrets, Rockface, Highlander and the Master of Ballantrae all being filmed here.

Loch Leven – 14 miles from Fort William
Scenes from the films Braveheart and Rob Roy were filmed in and around the area. Situated between Ballachulish and Kinlochleven, like many other locations in the area, this also has stunning scenery.

Glen Nevis – 1 mile from Fort William Centre
This glen with its stunning mountains, Ben Nevis and the River Nevis is an ideal place for the film producers so much so that large parts of Braveheart, Harry Potter, Highlander 3, Kidnapped, Restless Natives, Rob Roy, Quest for Fire and Rockface have all been filmed here.

Cille Choirill Church – Roy Bridge – 12 miles from Fort William

A 15th century church, which was restored, and re-opened in 1932. Shots of the church were used in Monarch of the Glen. You can view the church by obtaining the key from the gatekeeper's house at the bottom of the hill.

Cia – Aig Falls – 18 miles from Fort William

Nearby Achnacarry Castle at the end of The Dark Mile. Beside a small bridge over the river Cia-Aig is a waterfall and pool known as the Witch's Cauldron. Shots of this place were used for the film Rob Roy.

BEST WALKS IN THE AREA

The Lochaber area is surrounded by mountains and glens and is a place that many people go to for walking holidays. Many people visit this area for the spectacular scenery, as well as to climb Ben Nevis. Some may prefer short walks by the river, **photo 3.**

I have included four walks in this book, which I consider the best in the area. Walk No.4 Ben Nevis should only be attempted if you have suitable clothing and are reasonably fit. Walk No.2 Steall Falls is the easiest and a very popular walk.

All the walks can be quite strenuous in parts, **photo 22,** and should only be undertaken in reasonable conditions and wearing boots and appropriate clothing. It may be a nice, warm day in the glen, but as you ascend, it can be high winds and very cold on the summit of any of the mountains.

The recommended map for the area is O.S. No.392
Ben Nevis & Fort William

The Nevis Code

- Take your litter with you
- Keep dogs under close control
- Leave gates as you find them
- Do not damage anything – trees, buildings or historic sites
- Do not light fires
- Do not disturb wild birds, animals or plants
- Do not pollute watercourses
- Drive slowly especially on single-track road
- Park responsibly and not in passing places

Walk 1 - Cow Hill Mast (height 278m)
Start/Parking - Glen Nevis Visitor Centre GR. 122729
Distance - 5.8km (3.6 miles)   Time to allow – 2¼ hours
Terrain - Very steep ascent and descent for 750m on a well-defined path
Comment – A steep ascent to start but levels out at the top. Worth the effort. Ensure you have some spare warm clothing to put on at the summit.

1. Turn left out of the Glen Nevis Visitor Centre car park, and cross with care, walk for 230m to an entrance leading to The West Highland Way at the forest.

2. Turn right here, a small sign denotes the route along a straight path between fields for 120m, to a kissing gate at the entrance to Nevis Forest.

3. Walk up the short path between trees to meet a wider track, which you cross over then start ascending steeply up some steps that have a handrail at the side.

4. Continue on this steep ascent on a well-defined path through the forest to a kissing gate then on to a green post, which marks a turning off to the right leading to Cow Hill mast.

5. Turn right at the green post keeping on the stony path for 1.4km, crossing a stile then continuing on the undulating track leading to the mast, which you may see ahead, cloud permitting.

6. When you reach the mast, take care in low cloud, and do not venture too far away from the mast itself. Good views of Fort William and the surrounding area abound from here, **photo 12.**

7. Return on the same route to the Visitor Centre remembering to turn left at the green post and taking extra care on the descent.

Walk 2 - Steall Falls

Start/Parking – End of the road at Upper Falls car park GR. 168691 (Lock valuables in car boot).

Distance - 6km (3.7 miles)   Time to allow - 1½ hours

Terrain - Grass/stone path can be slippery when wet.

Comment - A pleasant walk with good views of the river and waterslide. The walk culminates in the spectacular Steall Falls waterfall in this hanging valley. This walk is not to be missed!

1. Starting from the end of the road at Upper Falls car park where the road stops. Just before the car park you pass an impressive water slide cascading down the mountainside on your left.

2. The path can be very slippery when wet. Initially the path is stony and rutted but well defined as you walk parallel with the river below in the Glen.

3. The path crosses two small waterfalls coming down the mountainside on your left. It may be difficult walking over the wet stones for part of the route here.

4. Cross another small waterfall, where looking down into the Glen you can see the river racing over the rocks on its journey down the Glen. Take care on the path as there is a steep drop off to your right.

5. You come to a high point on the path then you descend to a wooden platform before ascending over it. Hold the handrail as you pass.

6. Rounding a bend in the path you see a spectacular waterfall, **photo 7,** dropping into the river at the far end of this hanging valley.

7. At the far end of this valley on the opposite side of the river is a mountain rescue bothy. A rope bridge gives access to it. You have good views of Ben Nevis from here as you perhaps stop for a picnic before retracing your steps back to the car park.

Walk 3 - Dun Deardail Fort
Start/Parking - Glen Nevis Visitor Centre GR. 122729
Distance - 8.2km (5.1 miles)   Time to allow - 2½ hours
Terrain - Good forest track ascending gradually then a
short path to the fort with two short but steep ascents.
Comments - Another walk with spectacular views
throughout. Demanding in parts on the upper section.

1. Starting at the door of the Visitor Centre walk round to the road, turn left, walking for 230m to a sign on the opposite side pointing to The West Highland Way.
2. Turn right here along a straight path, to a kissing gate. Go through; ascend to a wide track with a small waymark sign again to The West Highland Way.
3. Follow this sign turning left to walk 700m to another sign at a fork in the track.
4. Turn off to the right following the sign and ascend through the forest on The West Highland Way. In the upper stages you go around two sharp bends on the track to a waymark post with a yellow arrow pointing along a narrow path to your right.
5. Ascend this path to a deer fence with a stile.
6. Go over, turning left along a line of trees on a narrow undulating path to the fort remains. The views from the summit are outstanding in all directions.
7. Retrace your steps, walking back through the forest to where your wide track joins another wide track at the lower end of the forest.
8. Turn right here walking for 400m to a metalled road section before turning left along a narrow path leading to a kissing gate.
9. Walk through then go between the houses onto a metalled road leading down to the main road beside the Glen Nevis Restaurant.
10. Turn left at the main road and walk for 1.1km on the footpath to the Visitor Centre.

Ben Nevis Facts

The path to the summit of Ben Nevis was originally built as a pony track to service the observatory and the hotel, which are now in ruins. The observatory was operational between 1883-1904. Surprisingly there have been a number of cars that have actually driven to the summit, no doubt with a lot of help. The highest war memorial in Britain is also situated on this summit. The views from here are breathtaking in all directions.

Walk 4 - Ben Nevis
Start/Parking - Glen Nevis Visitor Centre GR. 122729
Distance - approx 9 miles   Time to allow - 6½ hours
Terrain - Stony, rocky and uneven steep path for most of the way.
Take the A82 Inverness road then at the sign to Glen Nevis at the Nevis Bridge roundabout go straight across. From the roundabout it is 1.2 miles to the Glen Nevis Visitor Centre. **Park in the free car park here.** Near the car park is a pedestrian suspension bridge crossing the River Nevis, **photo 3.** A sign points to Ben Path. Follow this, passing a guesthouse. The visitor centre is now opposite. A sign states 'Ben Path', going over three wooden steps. Ascend for 150m then over two steps, going straight ahead. As you ascend you have a good view of Glen Nevis Caravan & Camping Park behind you. The path is stony, uneven and ascends steeply. Continue on this path, which eventually joins another path that ascends steeply from the right. You soon cross over a wooden platform bridge on the main path ascending Ben Nevis, which is known as The Tourist Route. The path is very stony and more uneven on this section. Approximately 80m further up is a seat on a bend in the path. You come to a metal bridge and this point affords good views of Glen Nevis.

Cross a small burn running down a gully, the path here is hard mud, interspersed with stones as it winds up the hillside. The path turns sharp left then right, followed by steps up a steep rock outcrop. A metal bridge spans a gully; again there are good views. The sound of a fast flowing burn running down another gully can be heard. A natural spring escapes from the hillside so the path is usually wet here.

A stone outcrop and another metal bridge with a waterfall beneath is crossed. The path then ascends steeply. You ascend between the two mountains with a burn on your right. It is called Red Burn in English. While ascending the side of the mountain burn you come to a sign saying Conservation Area. The path twists left and right as you approach the loch halfway up the mountain. The path levels out a little here with springs and melting snow making it wet in places. The area is open with a large expanse of grass. Lochan Meall an t-Suidhe is on the left.

Follow the path as it turns right and uphill again. Some piles of stones and a section of wall mark the path. Go immediately right there. It is important to note that the path going straight on leads to the area climbers' use.

Cross a small stream, which runs down the path. There are good views over the other mountains, **photo 23.** To your right there are some steep drops off. Cross over another burn where walkers usually stop for refreshment. Approaching the summit you can see down the glen to the youth hostel. Loch Linnhe is in the distance.

The final ascent is very rocky and uneven, **photo 22,** with loose stone and scree. As you approach a gully the route bends round sharp right on the scree path. You should see the mountain rescue hut 400m away in front. Near the summit the small stone path levels out, **photo 24.** Quite often, up to mid summer, this area is covered in snow.

You should see piles of stones on your ascent as you proceed, if there is no snow. Follow your path carefully if there is snow, it is important to stay on the path.

Immediately before the summit take extreme care of the sheer drops over the edge of the mountain, down the infamous Gardyloo Gully, Tower Gully and No.2 Gully. Stay on the path watching for snow overhangs, which can be deceiving. The gully just before the flat plateau summit is close to the path, so keep right, heading for the ruins of the observatory, which date back to Victorian Times.

On reaching the summit you have excellent views in all directions (cloud permitting). There is a triangulation pillar, number S1595 and emergency shelter. A cross with a cairn and plaque states it is Britain's highest War Memorial. It is the Fort William Dudley/Worcestershire Cairn of Remembrance.

After resting for a short time on the summit you may find the cold penetrating the body. This is now the time to start your descent to warmer and more sheltered areas. Retrace your steps down the mountain following the route you ascended.

N.B. **Ben Nevis should be treated with respect at all times. At over 4,000ft the weather on top can be very unpredictable.**

You should carry a map of Ben Nevis, and appropriate warm clothing. There are many loose stones on the path all the way to the top so wear walking boots or strong shoes. Carry a small rucksack with food, drinks and spare clothing. **Do not walk in jeans and t-shirt!** Stay safe and dress appropriately.

After walking Ben Nevis, you may like to walk the highest mountains in England and Wales at a later date. The recommended book to accompany you is The National 3 Peaks Walk, ISBN 1-903568-24-2 Price £6.95 and is obtainable from book and outdoor shops. The route to the summit of all three mountains is clearly explained, together with photographs, facts and figures about all three areas.

USEFUL INFORMATION

Recommended Maps
O.S. Explorer No.392
Ben Nevis & Fort William (1:25,000)

Weather Information
Ben Nevis Area   01397 705922
General Weather Web site
www.metoffice.gov.uk
(Click on mountain weather)

Grid References/Walk times for Ben Nevis
Glen Nevis Visitor Centre   GR. 122729
Halfway point on main path, near Lochan Meall
Ant-Suidhe GR. 147724
Emergency shelter, Ben Nevis summit GR. 166713
Visitor Centre start to Summit $3\frac{3}{4}$ hours
Summit to Visitor Centre $2\frac{3}{4}$ hours
Walk times may vary depending on fitness, weather
conditions and size of group.

Visitor/Tourist Information Centres
E mail info@host.co.uk
Glen Nevis Visitor Centre   01397 705922
Fort William T.I.C Information Line   0845 2255121
Ballachulish Visitor Centre   01855 811866
Kingdom of Scotland Visitor Centre
Spean Bridge   01397 712999

Fort William Taxi Service
Jenny Keane – Clansman Taxis   01397 703334
                                     01809 501411

Campsite
Glen Nevis Caravan & Camping Park   01397 702191
Glen Nevis
Fort William

Youth Hostel
Glen Nevis Youth Hostel   01397 702336
Glen Nevis

The following selection of accommodation is not arranged in any order of priority. All are within Fort William and Glen Nevis area.

Self Catering Chalets
Margaret Ferguson   01397 705905
'Harland'
Glen Nevis
Fort William PH33 6ST
ferguson@glennevis1.freeserve.co.uk

Bed & Breakfast
Constantia House   01397 702893
Fassifern Road
Fort William PH33 6BD
derek.walker61@btinternet.com

Corrie Duff Guest House & Holiday Cottages
Corrie Duff   01397 701412
Glen Nevis
Fort William PH33 6ST

'Glenfer'   01397 705848
Glen Nevis
Fort William PH33 6PF
stay@glenfer.com
www.glenfer.co.uk

Attractions

Crannog Cruises	01397 700714
Nevis Range Cable Cars	01397 705825
Ben Nevis Distillery	01397 702476
Ben Nevis Highland Centre	01397 704244
West Highland Museum	01397 702169
Lochaber Leisure Centre	01397 704359

Churches in Fort William

Church of Scotland
Free Church of Scotland, West End
St. Andrews, (Episcopal.)
United Free Church of Scotland
St. Mary's Roman Catholic, Belford Rd

Supermarkets in Fort William

Safeway, beside the railway station
Tesco, beside St. Andrews Church on the High Street

Leisure Centres

Lochaber Leisure Centre on Belford Rd. Pool, sauna, fitness suite, squash & climbing wall.   01397 704359
The Nevis Centre, nearby the Safeway supermarket. Ten pin bowling, snooker, bar diner, coffee shop, sports hall, children's play area, concerts and other events.   01397 700707

Fort William Golf Club   01397 704464

Hospital

Fort William Hospital on Belford Road. At the time of writing this book, the hospital was facing closure. The next main hospital is Inverness.

Railway Station

Just off A82 nearby Safeway supermarket
Trains run by Scot Rail www.scotrail.co.uk 08457 48 49 50

Scottish Natural Heritage
www.snh.org.uk

Visit Scotland
0845 2255121

Public Transport Information for Fort William
0870 6082608

Police Station
At the west end of the High Street

Banks in Fort William
Halifax
Clydesdale Bank, cash machine
Royal Bank of Scotland
Post Office
Lloyds TSB

Public Houses in Fort William Centre

Crofter Bar & Restaurant
Alexandra Hotel
Nevisport Bar
Imperial Hotel Bar
Volunteer Arms Pub

Ben Nevis Pub
Grand Hotel Lounge Bar
Grog & Gruel
West End Hotel

Cinema in Fort William
01397-705095

Car Hire-Fort William
Easydrive Car & Van Rental   01397 701616
Vauxhall Car Rental   01397 703877

Doctors – Fort William
01397 703136
01397 703773
01397 702947

Dentists – Fort William
01397 702147
01397 702501

Hopefully you have used this book and visited many of the places mentioned. If you have walked any of the walking routes described and would like to walk other challenging routes, please visit Challenge Publications website at: -

www.chall-pub.fsnet.co.uk
or
www.challenge-publications.tk

After walking Ben Nevis, you may like a souvenir to mark the event. The author has produced a selection of items for sale, these include: - a certificate for climbing Ben Nevis, and desk calendar for 2006 and future years, showing photographs of the route up the Ben.

Due to low cloud on the summit you may not have any photographs. A CD with 173 superb photographs of the route up Ben Nevis, with many views from the summit is available. A CD is also available with 156 photographs of Fort William and Glen Nevis area. These will help you relive your memories of the area. They can be viewed on a PC or on a television via a DVD player. Photographs can be printed from them.

Full details are available **for all souvenirs** by sending for a current price list enclosing a S.A.E. to: -

Brian Smailes
Challenge Publications
7, Earlsmere Drive
Ardsley
Barnsley
South Yorkshire S71 5HH

Should you wish to comment on this book or give further information to help keep the book updated then please write to the address above or e-mail via the website. An acknowledgement will be given.

INDEX